YOU DON'T HAVE TO DIE AND GO TO HELL

God's Promise of Salvation

Dennis Wilson

STRAIGHT
TRUTH PRESS

Straight Truth Press

To the One Holding This Book

To the ones I love who are still running.
You're not too far.
You're not too late.
I wrote this because I couldn't stay silent.
And because I still believe you can come home.

To the prodigals, the doubters, and the ones still unsure.
I know what it's like to wander.
I know what it's like to wonder if grace could still reach you.
This book is proof that it can.
And that someone was praying you'd pick it up.

To the one standing at the edge of forever.
This is not a threat. It's an invitation.
You don't have to die in your sin.
You don't have to go to hell.
The cross is still enough.
And grace is still calling.

Table of Contents

Preface

This book wasn't written to win an argument or stir up controversy. It was written to tell the truth—**plainly, biblically, and urgently.**

I've seen too many walk away from the faith. Too many believe the lie that they're too far gone. And too many churches have stopped talking about what's really at stake.

Hell is real. Judgment is coming. But you don't have to go there.

My prayer is that these pages cut through confusion and bring clarity.

That they speak to the one who's wandered. That they awaken the one who's grown numb. And that they reach even one soul who thought grace could no longer reach them.

If you're holding this book, **God is not finished with you.**

Read it. Wrestle with it.
Most of all—respond.

Introduction

Most people believe in heaven. Fewer believe in hell. And almost no one thinks they're going there.

We live in a culture that avoids eternal things. We bury guilt under distractions. We chase comfort. We assume that if we "mean well," we're probably fine.

But the Bible doesn't leave us in that kind of gray. It draws sharp lines—for our sake, not our shame. And ignoring those lines doesn't make them disappear.

The title of this book might shock you. That's okay. It's meant to be honest.

And maybe someone gave you this book—a friend, a parent, a sibling, someone who cares about you deeply. **Please hear me:** they didn't give it to you to judge you or make you feel bad. They gave it to you because they love you.

I love you.

This book was hard to write—because some of the people I love most might be headed for hell.

That's not a small thing to say—and I don't say it to scare you. I say it because I don't want that to happen. And more than that, **God** doesn't want that to happen.

This is not a *"you can go to hell"* book. This is an *"I love you too much to stay silent"* book.

If your house were on fire, I wouldn't just wave from the sidewalk. I wouldn't just hope you'd notice and get out. I'd run in. I'd try to pull you out—even if it made you mad at me. That's what love does.

Because the truth is—**you don't have to die and go to hell.**

But many will. Not because God failed to make a way. But because people refuse it.

This book exists to say what too few are willing to say. Not to scare you. Not to shame you. But to show you who Jesus really is—and why He is the only way out.

Each chapter will walk you through **Scripture**. Not a devotional. Not church tradition. Not preacher talk.

God's Word.

And now—**it's yours.**

PART ONE: THE LIES THAT KEEP YOU TRAPPED

The things we believe that keep us from believing God.

Chapter 1
Hell Wasn't Meant for You
A wake-up call—because God still wants you.

Hell is real. And it's horrible. But it wasn't created for you.

If that surprises you, good. If it shakes something loose in your heart, even better.

Because before we go any further—before we talk about judgment, salvation, the cross, or the choices that lead to life or death—you need to know the truth:

God did not design hell with you in mind.

That may not be what you've heard.

Some preachers have thundered about hell as if God can't wait to send people there. Others avoid the topic altogether, as if pretending it doesn't exist will somehow soften God's image. But Jesus didn't do either.

He didn't use hell to scare people into shallow religion. He talked about it because He came to rescue people from it. He didn't avoid the subject because He knew the stakes. He knew where sin leads. And He knew the human heart—how stubborn, proud, and blind we can be when we think we're fine without God.

But even as He warned of hell, Jesus said something most people overlook— Something most churches fail to emphasize:

> *"Then he will say to those on the left, 'Depart from me, you who are cursed, into the eternal fire*

prepared for the devil and his angels!'" —
Matthew 25:41

Read that again: *prepared for the devil and his angels.*

That's where hell came from. It wasn't a trap set for sinners. It wasn't designed as a punishment for the human race.

God created it as a final sentence for the original rebellion— the one that began not in Eden, but in heaven.

Satan, once a glorious angel, turned against his Creator—and others followed him. Scripture doesn't speak of any chance for repentance. It simply says they were cast out and judgment was set. God prepared a place—not out of cruelty, but as the just response to rebellion in His presence.

It was justice, not wrath for wrath's sake.

***

But something happened. The same deceiver who led that rebellion in heaven whispered his lies into the heart of man.

In Eden, he questioned God's goodness.

"Did God really say…?"
"You won't die…"
"You can be like God…"

And humanity believed the lie.

We turned away. Not just Adam and Eve.

You. Me. All of us.

Sin wasn't a glitch in the system—it became the system. And the more we chose ourselves, the more we inherited the path of rebellion.

Not because God forced us there, but because we walked it on our own.

***

Here's the part most people miss:

God didn't just step back and let us fall.

He stepped forward to stop it.

He called to Adam, even after the fall. He covered their shame with garments. He pursued, warned, sent prophets, raised up a people, made a covenant, and promised a Savior.

And when the time was right, He sent His own Son—not to condemn the world, but to save it.

And still… many reject Him.

This is what brings us to the terrifying possibility of hell— Not as a punishment God enjoys, But as the destination we insist on when we ignore His grace.

***

Don't miss the heart of God here. Listen to His own words through the prophet Ezekiel:

> *"As I live"—this is the declaration of the Lord GOD—"I take no pleasure in the death of the wicked, but rather that the wicked person turn from his way and live."* — Ezekiel 33:11

God takes no pleasure in it.

None.

He's not some cosmic executioner. He's a Father, pleading with His children to come home. But love demands freedom. And freedom always comes with consequences.

That's why hell exists—Not because God is mean, but because God is just, and because real love gives you a choice.

***

People ask, **"How could a loving God send anyone to hell?"**

But that's not the right question.

The real question is: **"How could anyone walk past the cross and say, 'No thanks'?"**

Hell is not where people end up because God does not love them. It's where they go because they refused that love.

***

Imagine a man drowning in the ocean. A rescue boat comes, tosses a rope, and says, "Grab on! We've got you!"

But the man shakes his head. "I'm fine. I don't need saving."

Eventually, he goes under—Not because no one cared, But because he said no to the only thing that could save him.

That's hell.

Not a mistake. Not a technicality. Not a place for people who didn't try hard enough.

It's the end result of someone who refused to be rescued.

***

And yes—God will honor that decision. As painful as it is, He will not override your will. You were created in His image. That means **your choice matters.**

Heaven is not for the "good people." Hell is not for the "bad people."

Heaven is for the forgiven.
Hell is for the stubborn.

***

Hell was never meant for you. But if you reject the only way out—If you ignore the blood of Jesus, If you silence His Spirit, If you cling to your pride until your final breath—

You are choosing what God never intended.

It's like locking yourself in a prison cell and throwing away the key—Even while a Savior is standing there saying, **"I already opened the door."**

***

So now the question becomes personal.

Not: **"What kind of God would send people to hell?"**

But: **"What kind of person hears this truth and still walks away?"**

God has done everything. He's warned you. He's pursued you. He's loved you.

He has not given up on you.

You don't have to die and go to hell. But if you do, It won't be because God wanted it. It will be because you wouldn't let Him save you.

***

This book is not about fear. It's about freedom. And that freedom begins with truth.

Let this truth sink in: Hell was never meant for you.

But Jesus? He was.
And He still is.

Chapter 2
I Am Too Far Gone
When guilt tells you you're beyond forgiveness—and grace says you're not.

It's a quiet fear, isn't it? It usually doesn't come with shouting or drama. It slips in like a whisper late at night. After the guilt. After the tears. After the moment you thought, *God could never forgive this.*

You sit with your thoughts and tell yourself what you've come to believe is true: **"I'm too far gone!"**

***

Maybe no one knows the whole story. Maybe you were baptized once. Maybe you even served in church.

You knew the truth, tasted it, maybe even preached it. And now? You carry your past like a weight chained to your soul, dragging it behind you every time you try to move toward God again.

You've convinced yourself that grace has a limit. That you blew your shot. That what you did was too dark, too shameful, too much. You don't say it out loud, but deep down, you believe it:

God might still love people.
But He doesn't love me.
Friend, that's a lie.
And we need to drag it into the light.

***

Let's start here: **sin is serious.**

We don't minimize that in this book. This isn't grace that winks at rebellion or shrugs at disobedience.

Sin separates. Always has.

The moment Adam and Eve disobeyed in the garden, they felt it. The loss of closeness. The hiding. The shame. It was instant.

But here's the part we miss: **God came looking for them.**

He didn't wait for them to fix it. He didn't demand that they find their way back. He came walking in the cool of the day, calling out, **"Where are you?"**

That's the heart of God—even when we're hiding.

***

Let's talk about David.

He wasn't just some guy. He was God's anointed king. A man after God's own heart. A worshipper. A warrior. A leader of God's people.

And then… Bathsheba. Lust. Adultery. Deception. Murder.

He broke every line. Shattered every expectation. And for a while, he thought he had gotten away with it. Until the prophet Nathan showed up with a story.

A story that ended with these four words:

> *"You are the man."*
> — 2 Samuel 12:7

David didn't run. He didn't explain it away. He didn't say, "But I'm king."

He broke.

> *"Against You—You alone—I have sinned,"* he cried in Psalm 51. *"Wash me... blot out my rebellion... create in me a clean heart, God..."*

And what did God do?

He forgave him. **Fully.**

Even though there were consequences, David's soul was restored. His prayers were heard. His calling wasn't canceled.

You haven't gone further than David. And even if you had— **God's mercy reaches further still.**

***

Peter is another name we need to say.

He walked on water. He saw the transfiguration. He declared Jesus was the Messiah.

And then he denied Him—not once, not twice, but three times. Cursing, swearing, lying—while Jesus was being beaten just feet away. And when the rooster crowed, Peter wept bitterly.

Shame has a sound to it, doesn't it? It's the sound of weeping when you realize you betrayed the One who loved you most.

But did Jesus write him off?

No.

After the resurrection, Jesus didn't just appear to Peter—**He restored him.**

"Do you love Me?" He asked. Three times. Possibly one for each denial.

And then came the call:

    "Feed My sheep." — John 21:17

Not only was Peter forgiven—**he was recommissioned.** He preached the first gospel sermon at Pentecost. Three thousand souls were saved that day.

So don't you dare say you've gone too far.

Not when Peter stood on a pulpit built from the ashes of his failure.

***

What about you?

Maybe your story is ugly. Maybe it's the abortion no one knows about. Maybe it's the affair. The addiction. The secret. The moment you knew what was right and chose the opposite.

You think your sin makes you the exception to the gospel. But the cross didn't come for exceptions.

It came for sinners.

And you still qualify.

If you did not still matter to God, you wouldn't be reading this. If His mercy were finished, your heart wouldn't be broken.

Conviction isn't evidence that God gave up on you— it's evidence that He hasn't.

You don't feel guilt because you're rejected. You feel it because the Spirit is still drawing you back.

The enemy shames. But God calls.

***

Paul called himself the "worst of sinners." He murdered Christians. He led the charge against the church. But when Jesus met him on the road to Damascus, He didn't destroy him. He saved him. He gave him a mission. A new identity. A name known around the world.

Paul didn't earn that. He didn't deserve it.

And neither do you. That's what makes it grace.

***

So here's the truth:

You are never too far gone. You've just been going the wrong direction.

And guess what? **God allows U-turns.**

Repentance isn't groveling. It's not working off your shame. It's not proving yourself.

It's turning.

It's hearing the voice of the Father saying, **"Come home,"** and dropping your excuses long enough to believe that maybe—just maybe—He still wants you.

And He does.

> *"Return to Me," says the LORD, "for I have redeemed you."* — Isaiah 44:22

That word **"redeemed"**? It means *bought back*.

You were His once. You left. And now He's saying, *I still paid the price.*

***

Don't tell yourself this book isn't for you.

Don't sit on the back row of God's kingdom and say, **"I'll never belong again."**

Don't chain yourself to a lie that God never spoke over you.

You may have fallen. You may have walked away.

But hear this:

You are not too far.
You are not too dirty.
Not too broken.
Not too stained.
Not too late.

Jesus didn't just die for the sins you committed before you knew better.

He died for the ones you committed after.

The ones you said you'd never do again. The ones you hate the most. The ones you still remember when everything else goes quiet.

And He still says:

Come.

Chapter 3

I Was Baptized...Then Blew It

Why falling after your baptism doesn't mean God is done with you.

Some scars don't come from ignorance. They come from disobedience. They come from knowing better—and doing it anyway.

This chapter is for the one who stood in the water, fully convinced that life would never be the same...and then, little by little, or maybe all at once, fell right back into the old life.

Maybe it was fast. Maybe it took years. But you woke up one day and realized:

I'm not who I said I would be.

And that baptism—the one you remember so clearly—now feels like a lie. The clean start feels dirty again. The joy is gone. You still believe in God, sort of, but you wonder if He's given up on you. Because you blew it.

And it wasn't just a stumble. It was sin.

Real sin. Willful sin. Shameful sin.

Sin committed by someone who once stood before God and said, *"I'm Yours."*

You still carry the memory of those waters. Maybe you remember the tears. The relief. The hope. The moment your past was buried. The moment the guilt washed off your skin.

The joy of starting new. But somewhere along the way, you started going back.

Maybe you felt clean for the first time. You thought you'd never go back. But life caught up. Or sin pulled hard. And now that moment feels far away—like it happened to someone else.

***

Let's tell the truth here. This isn't a surface issue.

People who've never been baptized, who've never committed to Jesus, can hear the gospel and say, *"Maybe I'll believe."*

But you?

You're haunted by it.

Because you already believed. You already said yes. You already made a vow. You already experienced grace.

So when you fall after that—it cuts deeper. It doesn't just feel like sin. **It feels like betrayal.**

Like Peter.

He didn't just make a mistake. He denied Jesus, after walking on water. He said, *"I don't know the man"*—after seeing Him shine on the mountain. And it wasn't a private failure. It was public. Loud. Final.

But when Jesus rose, what did He say?

"Go tell My disciples—and Peter." — Mark 16:7

Did you catch that?

And Peter.

Jesus didn't erase him. He called him by name. And not to scold him. Not to say, "I told you so." He called Peter back to remind him: **You still belong to Me. And I'm not done with you.**

***

So what happens when someone is baptized and then sins again?

It's a question Christians have struggled with since the very beginning. In the early church, some people believed you couldn't be forgiven after baptism. That your first chance was your last chance.

But that's not what the New Testament teaches.

First John was written to believers—**baptized believers**. People who had already confessed Christ and joined His body.

And here's what John says:

> *"If we walk in the light as He Himself is in the light, we have fellowship with one another, and*

the blood of Jesus His Son cleanses us from all sin."
— 1 John 1:7

"If we confess our sins, He is faithful and righteous to forgive us our sins and to cleanse us from all unrighteousness."
— 1 John 1:9

***

Did you see it?

The blood of Jesus doesn't stop cleansing just because you've already been washed.

Baptism is your burial and resurrection with Christ—It is the **beginning** of your life in Him. But life doesn't mean perfection. And forgiveness doesn't run on a timer.

Yes, you were cleansed. Yes, you were made new. **And yes— you still need grace every single day.**

Baptism is not a guarantee that you'll never sin again. It's a declaration that you're dead to your old life— And when you fall, you get back up not in your own strength, but **in His**.

***

Now, some people swing too far the other way. They say, *"Well, I was baptized, so I'm good no matter what."*

That's not faith. That's presumption.

God is not mocked. The call to follow Jesus is real— And so is the call to repent when we wander.

But if you're reading this, you're not mocking Him. You're mourning.

And that tells me something. It tells me the Holy Spirit hasn't stopped working in you. It tells me the enemy may have knocked you down, but he didn't silence your soul. It tells me your failure, as real as it is, **is not final.**

***

Think about the prodigal son.

He didn't stumble into sin. He ran into it with eyes wide open. He left the Father. Took the money. Spent it all. Woke up in a pigsty covered in filth.

And what did he say?

> *"I will go home. I will tell my Father, 'I have sinned.'"*
> — Luke 15:18

That was repentance. Not emotion. Not groveling. Just the honest return of someone who remembered what he left behind.

And when he came home?

The Father didn't lecture him. Didn't shame him. Didn't make him wait.

He ran.

He embraced him while he was still dirty. He restored him while he was still unworthy. He called for the robe, the ring, the feast.

> *"My son was dead, and is alive again. He was lost, and is found."* — Luke 15:24

. ***

Do you remember what you felt when you came out of the water? That joy? That lightness?

That's not lost forever. That joy doesn't come from a perfect track record. **It comes from knowing you're home.**

You've been far off. But you're not too far gone. You blew it. **And God still wants you.**

***

This isn't about repeating your baptism. It's about coming back to the One who once washed you, sealed you, and still calls you His.

You don't need a second ceremony. You need a second wind.

You need to remember that the blood that washed you once **still flows**. The tomb is still empty. The arms of the Father are still open.

***

So here's what I'm telling you:

You were baptized… and you blew it.

Now come home.

God is not looking for perfect people. He's looking for sons and daughters who know they need grace and aren't too proud to take it.

Jesus didn't die for the version of you that gets everything right. He died for the one reading this right now. He died for the one who knows better—and still hopes it's not too late.

You don't have to die and go to hell. And you don't have to live in shame, either.

Not anymore.

Chapter 4
I Don't Feel Forgiven
When your emotions contradict the promise of the cross.

Forgiveness is central to the Christian faith. We are told that God forgives sins. We are assured that if we confess, He is faithful to forgive. We hear this. Many of us even preach it to others. But when it comes to our own hearts, we often find ourselves asking:

"If I am forgiven, why don't I feel like it?"

This is not a shallow question. It's not a matter of low self-esteem or emotional immaturity. It is a real spiritual and theological problem that touches many believers—especially those who have fallen after conversion or who carry the weight of serious past sins.

They know the words of Scripture, but those words seem to echo in a room that stays emotionally cold.

What we need here is not comfort. We need clarity.

What does God's Word say about forgiveness? And how should we understand the gap between what is promised and what is felt?

Let's begin with what the Bible teaches.

***

Forgiveness Is a Legal Declaration, Not an Emotional Event

In Scripture, forgiveness is often described in legal terms. A debt is erased. A record is wiped clean. A verdict is declared: **not guilty**.

This is not a feeling. It is a status.

> *"Therefore, since we have been justified by faith, we have peace with God through our Lord Jesus Christ."* — Romans 5:1

The word *justified* means to be declared righteous in God's courtroom. It is not dependent on the sinner's emotional state. God does not wait to see how sorry we feel. He looks at the blood of His Son and counts us righteous because the penalty has been paid.

When we confess our sins, God does not conduct an emotional assessment. He does not require a certain level of regret or sorrow before forgiveness is extended.

Instead, He looks to the finished work of Christ, and on that basis, He forgives.

> *"If we confess our sins, He is faithful and righteous to forgive us our sins and to cleanse us from all unrighteousness."*
> — 1 John 1:9

This is an objective statement. It is grounded in **God's character**—His faithfulness and righteousness—not in our emotional response.

To believe otherwise is to put more trust in our feelings than in God's truth.

***

Why Doesn't Forgiveness Always Feel Real?

There are several reasons a forgiven person may not feel forgiven. Most of them come from **confusion—not rebellion**.

Let's examine them carefully.

***

1. We equate forgiveness with the removal of consequences.

Sometimes a person confesses sin and receives God's forgiveness, but the consequences remain.

A marriage remains strained.
A reputation is damaged.
A legal record still exists.

These consequences are painful, and because they linger, we assume forgiveness has not occurred. But this is not a biblical conclusion.

King David was forgiven for his sin with Bathsheba and the murder of Uriah:

"The Lord has taken away your sin; you are not going to die."
— 2 Samuel 12:13

But also:

"The sword shall never depart from your house."
— 2 Samuel 12:10

Forgiveness and consequence are not the same thing. God may allow consequences to remain even while He fully removes the eternal penalty of sin.

***

2. We expect an emotional experience.

In many Christian traditions, forgiveness is often associated with tears, joy, or a sense of relief. While these feelings are not wrong, they are not required.

Scripture never says, *"You will know you are forgiven by how you feel."* Instead, we are called to believe God's promise.

A person who confesses sin and turns to Christ in faith is forgiven—**whether they feel it or not.**

It is a matter of God's integrity, not our emotions.

***

3. We misunderstand the nature of guilt.

There are two kinds of guilt: **judicial** and **emotional**.

- Judicial guilt is objective. It is our standing before God apart from Christ.

- Emotional guilt is the sense of condemnation or shame we carry, even after being forgiven.

Scripture is clear that our judicial guilt is removed the moment we are justified by faith. But emotional guilt may remain—especially if we've sinned seriously, repeatedly, or publicly.

This emotional guilt is **not from God**. It is either from our own wounded conscience or from the accusations of the enemy.

"There is now no condemnation for those who are in Christ Jesus."
— Romans 8:1

No condemnation means exactly that. The court has rendered a verdict. God has not only dropped the charges—**He has declared the case closed.**

***

What Should You Do When You Don't Feel Forgiven?
The answer is **not** to chase after better feelings. It is to return to the truth, again and again, until the heart catches up to what the mind has been told.

Feelings are not the foundation of faith.

They are a result—sometimes delayed—of a life grounded in truth.

Just as a ship must be anchored during a storm, the believer must be anchored in what is written, not in what is felt.

If you've confessed your sin honestly, turned to Christ sincerely, and obeyed His call to be baptized for the forgiveness of your sins, then according to His Word—**you are forgiven.**

Not because you earned it. Not because you feel different. But because the blood of Jesus washes you clean at that moment—when you die with Him, are buried with Him, and are raised with Him through baptism.

Because God always keeps His Word.

***

What If You Continue to Feel Condemned?
Then you must reject those accusations as lies.

Scripture tells us that **Satan is the accuser of God's people**:

> *"The accuser of our brothers and sisters, who accuses them before our God day and night, has been hurled down."* — Revelation 12:10

He delights in reminding us of our worst moments. He wants to convince us that the cross was not enough.

But the blood of Christ speaks louder than the voice of the accuser. And God's verdict is final.

There is no more offering for sin. **Jesus has already paid in full.**

If you are in Christ, God is not waiting for more remorse. He is not waiting for a more dramatic confession. He is not holding forgiveness at a distance.

He has already given it.

***

Final Words

To be forgiven is to be declared innocent by the only Judge who matters. That verdict does not change because your emotions fluctuate.

If you are in Christ:

- Your sin is not ignored—it is **gone**.
- Your guilt is not overlooked—it is **erased**.
- Your soul is not tolerated—it is **adopted**.

And even if your feelings have not caught up yet, the truth still stands: **You are forgiven.**

Now walk in it.

Chapter 5
I Think I Missed My Chance
For the one who believes they waited too long.

There's a sinking kind of silence that settles into the soul of a person who believes they had a window, and missed it. Some people fear death. Some fear judgment. But others carry something more haunting: the belief that they already lost their one opportunity to be forgiven—that they had a season where God was calling, and they ignored it. And now that season is over.

They don't doubt the gospel is true. They just don't think it applies to them anymore.

They believe grace exists, but only for those who didn't wait too long.

If that's where you find yourself, then you need something more than encouragement. You need to understand what the Bible really says about God's patience, and whether the door of salvation truly closes before death.

Let's be precise. Let's deal with the theology, the fear, and the promise.

***

The Misunderstanding: Hebrews 6 and the Fear of No Return
One of the passages that troubles people most is found in Hebrews 6:

*"It is impossible to renew to repentance those
who were once enlightened, who tasted the
heavenly gift... and who have fallen away."*
— Hebrews 6:4–6, selected

At first glance, that sounds final. Many have read it and said,
"That's me. I knew the truth. I left it. And now it's too late."
But let's be careful with the text.

Hebrews was written to Jewish Christians who were tempted
to abandon Christ completely and return to Judaism—to go
back under the law, to reject Jesus as Messiah, and to place
their hope again in rituals and sacrifices that could never take
away sin.

The author's point is not that any Christian who sins after
salvation is doomed. His point is that if someone rejects
Christ altogether, even after knowing the truth, there is no
second Messiah coming. There's no new gospel to look
forward to. There's no other sacrifice beyond Christ.

This passage is not about the believer who stumbles and
repents. It's about the one who hears the gospel, turns away
permanently, and refuses to return.

If you are afraid you've missed your chance, and that fear is
drawing you back toward Christ—it is proof that you haven't
missed it. The very fact that your heart is tender, and not hard,
is evidence that the Holy Spirit is still working.

You don't fear being lost unless you want to be found.

***

The Nature of God's Patience

There's a line in 2 Peter 3 that corrects our fear with great clarity. Some in the early church were asking why Jesus hadn't returned yet—why God seemed slow to act. Peter responded:

> *"The Lord does not delay His promise, as some understand delay, but is patient with you, not wanting any to perish but all to come to repentance."*
> — 2 Peter 3:9

That is a statement of character.

God's slowness is not forgetfulness. It's mercy.

He withholds judgment not because He doesn't care—but because He still hopes more will repent.

Nowhere in Scripture does God promise unlimited chances. But He also never says there's a fixed number of times He'll call your name before He stops.

In fact, Jesus told a parable in Matthew 20 about workers who were hired at different hours throughout the day—some early in the morning, some at noon, and some just an hour before quitting time.

When the day ended, every worker who responded to the master's invitation received full payment. The ones who came late weren't scolded—they were welcomed.

The point is clear: **those who come, even late, are received.**

Real Examples of Last-Second Mercy

The thief on the cross is one of the clearest pictures of God's patience.

He lived a life worthy of condemnation. He admitted it himself. He had no opportunity to serve God, make amends, or start over. He had minutes left to live.

And still—he looked at Jesus and said, "Remember me."

Jesus replied with no hesitation:

> *"Today you will be with Me in paradise."*
> — Luke 23:43

That was not sentiment. It was the Savior's word.

This was not a man who got in because he was young and foolish. He was guilty, dying, with no future to offer.

His story tells us something essential: **You are not too late until your last breath is gone.**

***

But What If I Said No Too Many Times?

Some people fear they've resisted God too often—that their heart has grown too hard.

Scripture warns that our conscience can become seared *(1 Timothy 4:2)*, and that those who constantly suppress the truth can be handed over to a depraved mind *(Romans 1:28)*. These are sobering warnings. God does not guarantee repeated chances. Grace is never owed to us.

But again: if you are concerned that you've hardened your heart, that very concern is a sign that your heart is not hard.

Those who are truly past feeling don't grieve their distance from God. They dismiss it.

The broken soul says, "I want to come back, but I don't know if I still can."

To that soul, Scripture offers both warning and invitation:

> *"Seek the LORD while He may be found; call to Him while He is near."* — Isaiah 55:6

This is not a call to delay. It's a call to respond **now**. While He is near.

And the fact that you are reading this now, wrestling with the question, shows that He is near.

He has not walked away from you. He is not finished speaking. **But you must answer.**

***

Missing the Moment—or Misunderstanding It?

Often when people say, "I missed my chance," what they really mean is, "I didn't respond the first time. Or the second. Or the tenth."

They assume God only offers one window. But the Bible shows us again and again that He **pursues** the wandering.

Think of Jonah. God called him, he ran the opposite direction, and God sent a storm, a fish, and a second chance.

God may not chase forever. But He does chase longer than we deserve.

If you're reading this, **He is still chasing.**

The danger is not that God won't forgive you. The danger is that your shame and fear will keep you from accepting His forgiveness.

Don't let that happen.

Don't believe the lie that God slammed the door while you were still reaching for it.

He never said, *"Come only once."* He said, *"Come, all who are weary."*

If your heart is broken over sin, if your soul is aching for mercy— then this is not a missed moment.

It's your moment. Don't let it pass you again. He is still near.

So come.

Chapter 6

Success Isn't Salvation

When gaining the world costs you your soul.

Some lies come in the form of fear. Others come dressed as dreams.

This chapter is for the one who's been chasing something—fame, fortune, influence, applause—and thinks that if they just "make it," life will be fine.

Maybe it's sports. Maybe it's music. Maybe it's business. You were born with a fire, a talent, a drive. And you've chased it hard. You've sacrificed for it. You've prioritized it. You've shaped your whole life around it.

You don't hate God. You're not a rebel in the obvious ways. You just don't have time for Him. There are practices every week. Games on the weekends. Gigs and shows at night. Travel on Sundays. And your calendar has slowly pushed Christ to the edge.

You may not say it out loud. But the thinking is there:

"As long as I'm successful, I must be okay."

That's a lie. And it's a dangerous one.

Jesus said something that cuts through the applause and ambition:

> *"What good is it for someone to gain the whole world, yet forfeit their soul?"* —Mark 8:36

Read that again.

The whole world. Every trophy. Every dollar. Every record deal. Every scholarship. Every follower. Every title.

If you gain it all—and lose your soul—it's a bad trade.

You can be as big as the Beatles, as revered as Peyton Manning, as wealthy as Elon Musk, or as adored as Olivia Rodrigo—and if you die without Christ, **you still go to hell.**

And God doesn't want that.

***

You Were Made for More Than Applause
There's nothing wrong with working hard. With using your gifts. With building something good. But when the thing you build becomes the thing you bow to—it's not just dangerous. It's idolatry.

Scripture says:

> *"Do not love the world or the things in the world. If anyone loves the world, the love of the Father is not in him."*
> —1 John 2:15

This isn't about being poor. Or quitting your career. It's about your heart.

You were made for more than applause. More than a stage. More than a scoreboard.

You were made to know God—and without Him, all your success will rot in the grave right next to you.

***

Success Can Make You Comfortable. But It Can't Make You Clean.

Some people think their achievements will outweigh their sins. As if God will look at their résumé and say, "Well done."

But heaven isn't earned through success. And hell isn't avoided through fame.

Your soul doesn't care how many records you sell. Or how many touchdowns you throw. Or how many zeroes are in your bank account.

Your soul was made to live forever.

And there are only two destinations.

***

The Danger of Delayed Obedience

This is where it gets personal. You don't have to say "No" to God to end up in hell.

You just have to keep saying "Not yet."

That practice you rush to instead of church? That late night on the road that keeps you from the Word? That deal you make that silences your convictions?

Those little decisions form a pattern. And patterns form priorities. And priorities shape your soul.

The tragedy is not just that you could be lost. It's that you could be lost while surrounded by applause.

***

Teaching the Next Generation
Let's be honest:

It's not just our own souls we're shaping with our choices. **It's our kids'.**

When we raise children to believe that success is everything—when every week is packed with practices, lessons, workouts, rehearsals, games, and performances, all building toward the weekend's big event—we're not just managing a busy schedule.

We're making a statement.

We're teaching them that **God is optional.**

That worship is secondary. That the church is something we'll "get back to" after the season ends. That eternity can wait, but a scholarship can't.

And we may not say it with our words. But Jesus said:

"Where your treasure is, there your heart will be also."
—Matthew 6:21

The treasure doesn't lie. If we spend our time, our money, and our energy chasing success—and give God what's left (if anything)—our kids will notice.

And they'll follow.

We may love our kids deeply—and still lead them straight into idolatry.

But it's not too late to make a different kind of statement.

What if success looked like raising children who knew Christ? What if the legacy wasn't a trophy wall—but a testimony? What if they saw you surrender—and decided to follow?

You don't have to be perfect. But you do have to be honest.

Because the next generation is watching—and they're learning what matters most from you.

You Don't Have to Walk Away Empty

Jesus wasn't speaking to atheists when He said those words in Mark 8. He was speaking to His disciples.

Because even followers can forget what matters most.

You might not be famous yet. You might not "have it all." But if you're chasing a dream at the expense of your soul, the outcome is the same.

God's not asking you to quit your job or kill your dreams.

He's asking you to stop bowing to them.

He's asking you to come home.

***

It's Time to Trade Up
What the world offers looks bright for a while. But it fades. Glory fades. Beauty fades. Money fades.

Christ doesn't.

The world offers a stage. Christ offers a cross. The world offers applause. Christ offers salvation. The world takes your soul and calls it a success. Christ saves your soul and calls it a miracle.

The decision is yours.

> *"What good is it to gain the whole world and lose your soul?"*

That's not a warning for someone else.
That's a question for you.

***

You Don't Have to Die and Go to Hell

You can have forgiveness instead of fame. You can have joy instead of success. You can have life instead of applause.

And it starts by laying down the idol you've been chasing—and picking up the cross.

The world may never clap for you again.

But heaven will.

PART TWO: THE TRUTH THAT SETS YOU FREE

Jesus didn't come to condemn you—but to rescue you.

Chapter 7

Jesus Took Your Place

A clear look at the cross, substitution, and the payment that saved you.

Forgiveness is not possible simply because God is nice. Forgiveness is possible because Jesus Christ willingly took your place—bearing in His body the full weight of judgment that your sins deserved.

This chapter is not about feelings. It is about facts—facts grounded in Scripture, secured in history, and essential to understanding what salvation actually is.

It is not enough to say, "Jesus died." Many people die.

It is not enough to say, "Jesus died for sins." Many people have died as martyrs or moral examples.

The gospel is not merely that Jesus died. It is that **Jesus died as a substitute**—in your place, for your guilt, under your judgment.

Without this, there is no gospel.

***

The Necessity of Substitution

Sin is not merely a personal failure. It is a violation of God's law and God's nature. Every sin is an act of defiance, an assault on God's authority, and an offense to His holiness.

Scripture describes sin not just as a weakness, but as **lawlessness** *(1 John 3:4)*, **rebellion** *(Isaiah 1:2)*, and **enmity against God** *(Romans 8:7)*.

Because God is just, He does not ignore sin. He does not sweep it aside. If He did, He would cease to be righteous. We rightly demand justice in our human courts; how much more should we expect it from the Judge of all the earth?

> *"He will by no means leave the guilty unpunished."* — Exodus 34:7

So how can a holy God forgive a guilty person without violating His own justice? Only by satisfying that justice **through a substitute**.

This is the central message of the cross.

***

What Happened on the Cross?

The New Testament writers do not describe the death of Jesus merely as a tragedy. They describe it as a **transaction**— a deliberate, divinely ordained act of substitution.

> *"He Himself bore our sins in His body on the tree."* — 1 Peter 2:24

> *"The Lord has laid on Him the iniquity of us all."* — Isaiah 53:6

"God presented Him as a propitiation through faith in His blood, to demonstrate His righteousness." — Romans 3:25

The word *propitiation* means that Jesus **absorbed the wrath** that was rightly due to sinners. He didn't deflect it. He didn't diminish it. **He took it.** Fully.

On the cross, Jesus was not simply suffering. He was **standing in your place**.

Not symbolically.
Not metaphorically.
Literally.

He was judged so you could be pardoned. He was condemned so you could go free. He was pierced, not as a martyr, but as a **substitute**.

***

The Innocent for the Guilty
Pilate stood Jesus before the crowd and offered to release one prisoner. They chose Barabbas—a convicted criminal. Jesus, the innocent one, was condemned.

That moment is more than politics. It is a **portrait**.

The guilty man went free. The sinless man took his place.

That's the gospel.

Not that good people get better. Not that bad people try harder. But that **guilty people go free** because the innocent Son of God takes their punishment upon Himself.

Every lash of the whip, every nail, every hour of agony was deserved—**not by Him, but by you**.

And yet, He did not resist. He did not speak in His own defense. He did not call angels to deliver Him.

He bore it all, willingly, because only in this way could **justice be satisfied and mercy extended**.

> *"Christ also suffered for sins once for all, the righteous for the unrighteous, that He might bring you to God."* — 1 Peter 3:18

Why This Must Be Personal

It is not enough to say, "Jesus died for the world." You must say, "Jesus died for me."

Your sin is not theoretical. Neither is Christ's sacrifice.

He did not die for the *possibility* of salvation. He died to **actually redeem** a people for Himself *(Titus 2:14)*.

If you are one of them, it means this: **Your sin has been paid for, in full.**

The debt is not postponed. It is erased. The wrath is not redirected. **It is gone.**

To reject this—whether through indifference, pride, or delay—is to say, in effect, *"I will carry my own judgment."*

But judgment is not light. The cross proves it.

If there had been any other way to deal with sin, the Father would not have sent the Son to endure such torment.

But there was no other way.

Jesus said:

> *"If it is possible, let this cup pass from Me."* — Matthew 26:39

But it was **not** possible.

The cup of wrath had to be drunk. And **He drank it—every drop**—so you could be forgiven.

***

What This Means for You
If Christ took your place, then:

- You have **no reason** to remain under guilt.
- No reason to try to **pay God back**.
- No reason to live afraid that He might still hold something against you.

To **doubt** the sufficiency of the cross is not humility. It is **unbelief**.

If Jesus really bore your sin, then **you don't have to**.

This is not a theory to ponder. It is a **truth to believe**—and a **foundation to build your entire life on**.

The cross wasn't just a symbol. It was the altar. And Jesus didn't just bleed—He bore the sentence. The verdict was guilty. The penalty was death. But Jesus stepped in—not as Judge, but as your Advocate.

He stood where you should have stood. He took what you deserved. And now the record is wiped clean. Not because justice was ignored— but because justice was satisfied.

Chapter 8
God Wants You

Not out of pity—but because He loves you, personally and intentionally.

It is one thing to believe that God forgives sin. It is another to believe that He wants you.

This chapter is not about proving God is capable of saving you. That has already been established. He is sovereign. He is holy. He is just. And He has provided the only sufficient sacrifice in His Son. All of that is true.

But here we are not asking whether God is able to forgive. We are asking whether God is willing. And more than that: **Is He willing… for me?**

Not for the world in general. Not for the innocent or the uninformed. Not for the clean or the church-raised or the doctrinally sound.

But for the person who is reading this now—perhaps ashamed, perhaps distant, perhaps numb—wondering not, *"Can God forgive?"* but *"Would He still want me even if He could?"*

***

God's Desire Is Not Hidden
Many people assume that God tolerates sinners out of obligation. That the cross was an act of duty, not desire. That Jesus went to the cross because it had to be done—not because He wanted us.

But Scripture paints a very different picture:

> *"God proves His own love for us in that while we were still sinners, Christ died for us."*
> —Romans 5:8

This is not reluctant mercy. This is love demonstrated in its most unfiltered form. And not after we improved. Not after we changed. Not after we apologized.

While we were still in rebellion—while we were enemies—God moved toward us.

> *"The LORD appeared to him from far away: I have loved you with an everlasting love; therefore I have continued to extend faithful love to you."*
> —Jeremiah 31:3

This verse is not about momentary kindness. It speaks of a love that precedes your existence. An eternal decision, not based on your behavior, but rooted in God's own character.

He does not save because you are lovable. **He saves because He loves.**

***

The Language of Invitation

Jesus did not speak to crowds with detached neutrality. His words were pointed. Personal. And full of invitation.

> *"Come to Me, all who are weary and burdened, and I will give you rest."* —Matthew 11:28

The phrase *"Come to Me"* is not theological theory. It is a relational appeal. Spoken not to saints, but to the weary. The burdened. The ones who had tried religion and still found no rest.

That invitation still stands.

Likewise, Jesus says:

> *"See! I stand at the door and knock. If anyone hears My voice and opens the door, I will come in to him and eat with him, and he with Me."* — Revelation 3:20

This verse has been sentimentalized in modern culture, but it is deeply serious. It was spoken not to unbelievers, but to a lukewarm church—one that thought it had everything it needed but had shut Christ out.

Still, He knocks. Still, He desires fellowship.

This is not the language of obligation. **It is the language of a God who wants to dwell with His people.**

***

God's Motive Is Love
This is not to say that love cancels holiness. It doesn't. God's love is not permission to live in sin. **But it is the reason He came to rescue us from it.**

John 3:16 is well known, but not well believed.

"For God so loved the world that He gave His one and only Son..."

Many read that verse and assume *"the world"* means the innocent parts—the potential, the future church, the ones who would believe. But the word means **humanity in its totality**.

God gave His Son not in response to our goodness, but in response to our need. He loved not the potential in us, but the people enslaved to sin.

Paul wrote it this way:

> *"Even when we were dead in our trespasses, He made us alive together with Christ..."*
> —Ephesians 2:5

Not weak. Not misguided. **Dead.** And still—He loved.

***

This Is Not Generic
God's desire is not generic. **It is personal.**

In John 17, when Jesus prays to the Father before His arrest, He says:

> *"I am praying not for the world, but for those You have given Me, because they are Yours."*
> —John 17:9

Later He adds:

"Father, I want those You have given Me to be with Me where I am..." —John 17:24

This is not indifference. **This is desire.**

If you belong to Christ, it is not because God was forced to accept you. It is because **He chose to.** Freely. Willingly. Purposefully.

Paul says that God predestined us *"in love"* and adopted us *"according to the good pleasure of His will."* —Ephesians 1:4–5

That phrase—**"the good pleasure of His will"**—means **God wanted to.** No external force compelled Him. He was not trapped by His justice or pressured by pity. **He wanted you.**

***

What About Those Who Struggle to Believe This?
Often it is those who know their sin best who struggle most to believe that God still wants them.

If that's you, consider this: **The greater the sin, the more clearly God's grace is displayed in forgiving it.**

> *"Where sin multiplied, grace multiplied even more."*
> —Romans 5:20

Paul does not say grace overlooks sin. **He says it exceeds it.**

This is not permission to sin more—Paul refutes that idea immediately in Romans 6. But it is assurance that your worst moments are not outside the reach of God's mercy—**and are not outside the bounds of His desire for you.**

***

The Father Does Not Merely Tolerate the Prodigal

When Jesus told the parable of the prodigal son, He was not sentimentalizing forgiveness. **He was teaching the nature of the Father.**

The son had wasted his inheritance. He had disgraced his family. He returned home rehearsing a speech, hoping only to be tolerated as a servant.

But the father ran to him, embraced him, clothed him, and celebrated him. And the son never even got to finish his apology.

This is how Jesus described God.

Not reluctant. Not restrained. Not calculating. **Eager.**

The Father is not ashamed to receive His children. He does not put them on probation. **He welcomes them fully—not because they have earned it, but because they are His.**

***

Final Clarity

You may still struggle to believe it. You may say, *"I don't feel wanted."*

But **feelings are not the test of truth**. Look at the cross. If God did not want you, He would not have crushed His Son in your place.

Look at the open grave. If God did not want you, Christ would not have risen to give you new life.

Look at the Scriptures. If God did not want you, He would not have spoken your name in the pages of His story—calling the lost, restoring the fallen, pursuing the rebel, cleansing the ashamed.

God does not save reluctantly. He saves because He wants to. And yes—He wants you.

Chapter 9

The Gift You Must Choose

Grace is free, but never forced. You must receive it.

There is no shortage of people who say they believe in God. They acknowledge His existence. They agree that Jesus died and rose again. They know what the Bible says about sin, grace, and judgment.

But agreement is not faith. Recognition is not reception. Salvation is not automatic.

The gospel is not something God installs in the background of your life. It is a gift—offered freely, but never forced. And like all gifts, it must be received.

***

Grace Requires a Response

Scripture presents the gospel in terms that make response inescapable. Over and over, it uses words like **come, believe, repent, receive, call upon, follow**. These are not passive verbs. They require movement.

> *"To all who did receive Him, He gave the right to be children of God, to those who believe in His name."* —John 1:12

Notice the condition: **to all who received Him**. Not to those who merely knew about Him. Not to those who heard sermons. Not to those who were religious. But to those who received Him.

Faith is not mental assent. It is surrender. It is trust. It is laying down your arms and submitting to the authority of Christ—not partially, but completely.

***

The Nature of the Gift

It is easy to misunderstand what kind of gift salvation is.

Some assume it is a kind of contract: you do your part, God does His. If you behave, He blesses. If you repent, He forgives. If you keep your end, He keeps His. But that is not a gift. That's a transaction.

Others assume it is a vague offer of goodwill: a blanket statement of forgiveness that requires no response at all. But Scripture does not support that idea either.

Salvation is a **covenantal gift**—freely given, but requiring a relational acceptance. You do not earn it. You do not add to it. But you must take hold of it.

To reject the gift is not neutral. **It is fatal.**

> *"Whoever believes in Him is not condemned, but whoever does not believe is already condemned, because he has not believed in the name of the one and only Son of God."*
> —John 3:18

The person who walks away from Christ is not postponing salvation. **They are rejecting it.** And that rejection carries consequences.

***

When Silence Says No

One of the most sobering truths in Scripture is that refusing to choose Christ is itself a choice. There is no neutral ground.

Jesus said:

> **"The one who is not with Me is against Me."** —
> Matthew 12:30

This is a hard word. Many would prefer a middle path. They say, *"I'm not against God. I'm just not ready."* But indecision is not safety. It is danger dressed up as delay.

I've known people who still say they believe in Jesus. They still pray — sometimes before meals, sometimes in crisis. They'll talk about how good the Lord has been to them.

But there's no church. No Scripture. No real surrender. They don't follow Jesus — they just remember Him.

And when you ask, they'll say, "I know I need to get back. I will. I just need to get things right first."

But it's been years.

And here's the sobering truth: The longer someone says "not yet," the more it starts to sound like "not ever." People don't usually reject God with a loud no. They just drift until He's a memory. And memories don't change lives.

Belief without surrender isn't salvation. And praying without following is just nostalgia.

***

Think of Israel at the border of the Promised Land. After all God had done—delivering them from Egypt, parting the Red Sea, feeding them in the wilderness—they stood before the land God had sworn to give them.

And they hesitated. They feared the enemies. They doubted the promise. And in doing so, they turned a moment of decision into forty years of judgment.

God called it rebellion.

> *"None of the men who have seen My glory and the signs I performed in Egypt and in the wilderness... will ever see the land I swore to give their ancestors."* —Numbers 14:22–23

Delay became disobedience. And disobedience brought judgment.

The same pattern remains. You may not say "no" to God with your mouth. But if your heart says, *"Not yet,"* **you are rejecting Him just the same.**

***

The Urgency of the Present
The New Testament uses urgent language to call for response:

"Now is the acceptable time; now is the day of salvation."
—2 Corinthians 6:2

This urgency is not manipulation. It is wisdom. You are not guaranteed tomorrow. You are not promised another opportunity.

The voice you hear today may grow fainter tomorrow—not because God retreats, but because the human heart grows dull when truth is ignored.

The same sun that melts wax hardens clay.

If the Spirit is drawing you now, that is not a sign to wait. It is a call to surrender.

The delay itself is a form of defiance—subtle, maybe, but deadly.

***

What It Means to Receive the Gift

To receive Christ is not a formula. It is not the repetition of certain words. It is the response of a broken, believing heart.

It includes **confession**—acknowledging that you have sinned, not just as a mistake, but as rebellion. It includes **repentance**—turning away from sin and self-rule. It includes **faith**—not just believing that Jesus is Lord, but trusting Him enough to listen and obey.

Faith means hearing the message about Christ, believing it's true, and acting on it. It means trusting that He died in your place, and that His resurrection is your only hope for real life.

But even beyond these, it includes a **transfer of allegiance**.

You are no longer your own. **You belong to Christ.**

> *"You are not your own, for you were bought at a price. So glorify God with your body."*
> —1 Corinthians 6:19–20

This is not a shallow agreement. **It is a surrender.**

***

Salvation Is Free—but Not Cheap
God does not charge you for grace. But that does not mean it is cheap.

It cost the life of His Son. It required the full outpouring of His wrath. It was the most costly gift ever given.

And it will cost you **your self-rule**.

You cannot cling to your sin and also receive salvation. You cannot love the darkness and walk in the light. **You must choose.**

***

The Choice Is Yours
This is not pressure. It is truth.

God will not force your hand. He has extended the gift. He has proven His love. He has invited you in.

But He will not drag you across the threshold.

You must come.
Not tomorrow.
Not when your life is cleaner.
Not after you *"feel"* ready.

Now.

Chapter 10
What Does God Want From Me Now?
How to walk in obedience after choosing life.

You've come to Christ. You've received the gift. You've confessed your sin, trusted in the cross, and surrendered your claim to self-rule. You're not trying to earn forgiveness anymore—you've obeyed the gospel. So now what?

That is a fair and necessary question. Because salvation is not the end of your story. It is the beginning.

God does not save you merely to rescue you from judgment. He saves you to reconcile you to Himself and to transform your life. He is not simply sparing you from hell. He is calling you into discipleship—a life of learning, growing, obeying, and following His Son.

You may be wondering what that actually looks like. Is it about church attendance? Bible reading? Giving money? Changing your habits?

Let's answer it directly—from Scripture, not from tradition or assumption.

***

You Were Saved for Relationship, Not Religion
When Jesus called people to follow Him, He did not give them a checklist. He said,

"Follow Me."
— Matthew 4:19; John 10:27

That phrase is central. Christianity is not about adopting a moral code. It is about being united to a living Person. When God saves a sinner, He does not simply give them a clean slate—He gives them Himself.

"God is faithful; you were called by Him into fellowship with His Son, Jesus Christ our Lord."
— 1 Corinthians 1:9

That word *fellowship* means ongoing communion—a life in relationship with Christ, rooted in obedience and sustained by His presence.

This is not mystical. It is daily. It is lived out through time in the Word, prayer, repentance, obedience, and participation in the life of the church.

God is not calling you to a performance. He is calling you to walk with Him.

***

You Were Redeemed to Reflect His Glory
Salvation is not only about what you are saved from. It is also about what you are saved for.

"For we are His workmanship, created in Christ Jesus for good works, which God prepared ahead of time for us to do."
— Ephesians 2:10

Good works are not the cause of salvation. But they are the result.

Your life is now meant to reflect the character of the God who saved you. This means a transformation—not just of behavior, but of desires, priorities, speech, relationships, and goals. You were not just cleansed from sin. You were set apart for a purpose.

This transformation is not instant. But it is real. It is the work of the Holy Spirit, who now dwells in you, teaching you to say no to sin and yes to righteousness *(Titus 2:11–12)*.

***

You Are Called to Obedience
We live in a culture that is suspicious of authority. But in Scripture, obedience is not a burden. It is the natural fruit of love.

> *"If you love Me, you will keep My commands."*
> — John 14:15

Obedience is not payment. It is your spiritual act of worship.

Now that you belong to Christ, your life is no longer your own. You are under new ownership. That means learning His commands, submitting to His authority, and growing in holiness—not to earn His love, but because you have received it.

This obedience is not vague. The New Testament is filled with concrete instructions about how believers are to live. They are to flee sexual sin, put away lies and slander, forgive others, bear with one another, pursue humility, submit to spiritual leaders, honor marriage, provide for their families, avoid greed, and serve the church.

You will not do this perfectly. But if your life does not begin to reflect increasing submission to God's will, you must ask whether your heart has truly been changed.

***

You Are Placed Into a Body

Salvation is personal. But it is not private.

When God saves you, He joins you to His people. The image used in the New Testament is the *body of Christ.* You are now part of it—connected to other believers, dependent on them, and called to live in fellowship with them.

> *"Now you are the body of Christ, and individual members of it."*
> — 1 Corinthians 12:27

This means that isolation is not an option. You are not meant to walk alone. God has designed the local church to be the place where you are taught, shepherded, corrected, encouraged, and equipped.

Being added to the church isn't something you do—it's something God does when you surrender to Christ. But living as part of a local church isn't optional. It's obedience. It's necessary. The New Testament assumes it. The early church practiced it. And your spiritual health depends on it.

***

You Are Not Finished

Sometimes people treat baptism like graduation. They believe they've arrived. But the New Testament speaks of salvation as a starting point—a new birth, a spiritual beginning.

> *"Like newborn infants, desire the pure milk of the word, so that you may grow up into your salvation."* —1 Peter 2:2

You will need to grow in understanding, endurance, humility, and faith. You will need correction. You will stumble. And you will be disciplined—because God is your Father now, and He trains His children *(Hebrews 12:5–11)*.

This process is not glamorous. It is lifelong. But it is also glorious. You are being conformed to the image of Christ— not instantly, but progressively, and one day, permanently.

***

What God Wants Now Is What He Has Always Wanted

He wants your trust. He wants your loyalty. He wants your attention. He wants your worship. He wants your whole life.

> *"Love the LORD your God with all your heart, with all your soul, with all your strength, and with all your mind."* — Luke 10:27

This has never changed.

And He does not leave you to figure this out alone. He gives you His Spirit to indwell you, His Word to instruct you, and His church to walk beside you.

He will finish what He started in you. But you must follow.

Chapter 11
Forgiven, But Not Untouched
When grace removes your guilt but not all the consequences.

Some people carry a quiet burden. Not because they don't believe God can forgive—but because they're still living with the aftermath of what they did before He did.

They've confessed. They've repented. They've come home. But the marriage is still tense. The trust is still broken. The past still echoes. The consequences remain.

And so the question creeps in:

"If I'm forgiven, why am I still suffering?"

That's what this chapter is about.

Let's say it clearly: **Forgiveness is real. But it doesn't always undo what sin has damaged.**

That truth isn't harsh — it's freeing. Because it helps you stop confusing the pain of consequences with the judgment of God. The pain might still be there. But the condemnation is not.

***

Forgiveness Is Immediate. But Healing Often Takes Time.

The Bible says:

> *"If we confess our sins, He is faithful and*
> *righteous to forgive us our sins and to cleanse us*
> *from all unrighteousness."* —1 John 1:9

That's not a feeling. That's a fact. **When God forgives, it's done.** No delays. No second opinions. No probation period.

You are not half-forgiven or partially restored. You are clean.

But that doesn't mean everything goes back to how it was.

Sometimes sin breaks things that don't get fixed right away. Sometimes not at all.

That doesn't make God less gracious. It means you live in a broken world where actions have impact.

***

David: Cleansed, Restored — But Scarred

King David knows this deeply.

After his sin with Bathsheba — adultery, deceit, and murder — he finally breaks. When the prophet Nathan confronts him, David doesn't argue. He confesses.

> *"I have sinned against the Lord,"*
> David says.

Nathan replies:

> *"The Lord has taken away your sin; you will not*
> *die. However, because you treated the Lord with*
> *such contempt in this matter, the son born to you*
> *will die."*
> —2 Samuel 12:13–14

God forgives David. No hesitation. No delay. But God doesn't erase all the consequences.

David's family falls into chaos. His public reputation crumbles. And the child born from his sin dies.

God isn't taking back His mercy. He is showing that even forgiven sin leaves a wake.

Forgiveness doesn't mean pretending it didn't happen. It means you no longer carry the guilt before God—but you may still carry the results in this life.

***

There's a man I know well. Years ago, in his younger life, he stepped outside of God's design for relationships. That choice led to a pregnancy. A child was born — an undeniable blessing from God.

But the relationship didn't last. The couple didn't marry. They went separate ways.

He repented. He confessed his sin. He knows he is forgiven.

But the consequences have lasted a lifetime.

His daughter grew up without her father in the home. Her mother did the best she could to raise her. And now, nearly forty years later, that man still lives with the pain of a relationship that was never built, a wound that never fully healed.

Not because God hasn't forgiven him.
God's grace is real, and he walks in it.

But the ache is real too. The regret. The distance. The silence.

Some consequences don't disappear. Some scars don't fade. And some pain may not lift until we are made new.

***

When Forgiveness Doesn't Erase the Memory
David says in Psalm 51:

> *"My sin is always before me."*

He doesn't say that before he's forgiven. He says it *after*. Even in grace, the memory doesn't always go away.

Proverbs says:

> *"The one who commits adultery lacks sense; whoever does so destroys himself. He will get wounds and dishonor, and his disgrace will never be removed."*
> —Proverbs 6:32–33

That's not saying forgiveness is unavailable. It's saying sin costs more than we realize — sometimes for the rest of our lives.

You can be free from guilt and still feel the grief. You can be right with God and still live with what went wrong.

That doesn't mean you're stuck in shame. It means you're honest about what sin really does.

***

Consequences Are Not Condemnation
So let's be clear:

You can be fully forgiven and still face consequences. You can be loved by God and still walk with a limp. You can be completely cleansed and still be picking up pieces.

None of that means God is angry with you.

Hebrews 12 tells us:

> *"No discipline seems enjoyable at the time, but painful. Later on, however, it yields the peaceful fruit of righteousness to those who have been trained by it."*
> —Hebrews 12:11

God isn't making you pay for what Jesus already covered. He is helping you grow into someone who knows grace more deeply than ever.

Some of the most humble, Spirit-filled people I know are the ones who have been forgiven much—but who never forget what their sin cost.

They don't live in guilt. They live in gratitude.

But they also live in wisdom.

***

When the Wound Doesn't Go Away
Forgiveness removes the guilt. But that doesn't mean you walk away untouched.

Just ask Jacob. After wrestling with God, he receives a new name — **Israel**. He walks away blessed. Chosen. Changed.

But he also walks away limping. Not because grace failed him. But because the encounter changed him.

The limp wasn't punishment. It was a reminder: he had met God — and he would never be the same.

Or think of the Israelites in the wilderness, bitten by serpents because of their rebellion. God doesn't take away the snakes right away. He doesn't erase the pain.

Instead, He tells Moses to lift up a bronze serpent on a pole — and everyone who looks in faith **lives** (Numbers 21:9).

They don't die. But they still carry the scars.

Grace doesn't cause the pain. Sin does. Life does. Our own rebellion does.

But grace meets us there. Grace **doesn't erase every scar** — but it keeps them from defining us. Grace **doesn't remove every limp** — but it walks beside us through every step.

***

Final Words
You are forgiven. That is finished. But the grace that saves you doesn't always fix everything around you.

While it changes **your standing** with God, it may not change **your situation**.

Forgiveness lifts the guilt. But it may leave a limp.

Still—don't mistake discipline for rejection. Don't confuse consequences with condemnation.

You are still His.

You may feel broken. But Jesus came for the broken. The poor. The wounded. The guilty. The ashamed.

That's who He read about in the synagogue. That's who He came to rescue. That's who He still restores today.

And if the scars you carry never fade in this life, they can still point to the One who carried all your sin on the cross.

You don't have to die and go to hell. But you don't have to live pretending sin was painless either.

You are forgiven. You are not untouched. But you are still His.

PART THREE: THE CALL THAT WON'T LET YOU GO

Even now, God is calling you back home.

Chapter 12

Why You're Still Breathing

Every day you're alive is mercy—and a call to respond.

You are still alive. That may seem obvious, but it is worth saying plainly. Your heart continues to beat. Your lungs fill with air. You woke up today in a world governed by God's providence. You have not yet died in your sin. You have not yet faced the judgment seat. You are still here.

The question is why.

If your sin is real, and God is holy, and judgment is certain—then why are you still drawing breath?

The answer is not chance. It is not luck. It is not the universe "giving you another day." It is mercy—plain, undeserved, deliberate mercy.

> *"Because of the LORD's faithful love we do not perish, for His mercies never end. They are new every morning; great is Your faithfulness."*
> — Lamentations 3:22–23

You have not slipped through the cracks. You have been spared on purpose.

God's mercy is not theoretical. It is visible every morning you wake up and realize that the door has not yet been closed. You are still breathing because God has not yet given you what you deserve.

And that raises a different kind of question: **What will you do with the time you've been given?**

***

Time Is Not an Accident

Every second that passes is a gift. Not because you've earned it, but because God has willed it. He upholds the universe by the word of His power (Hebrews 1:3). If He were to stop speaking, the world would cease to exist.

So when you wake up and feel the pull of your own heart, or the weight of conviction, or the call to come back to Him— that is not a coincidence. That is a mercy that was written into your very existence by a God who still wants you.

You were not owed this day. But you were given it. And with that gift comes responsibility.

***

The Patience of God Is Meant to Lead You Somewhere

Paul writes to the Romans:

> *"Do you despise the riches of His kindness, restraint, and patience, not recognizing that God's kindness is intended to lead you to repentance?"* — Romans 2:4

God is patient. But His patience is not passive. It is not weakness. It is not delay for the sake of delay. It is a strategic withholding of judgment, meant to produce a response.

He restrains His wrath so you will return to Him.

Every breath is an invitation. Every heartbeat is a summons.

When you put off repentance—when you say, "Later" or "Someday"—you are not pausing the plan. You are resisting the call.

And that resistance builds something. Paul continues:

> *"Because of your hardened and unrepentant heart, you are storing up wrath for yourself in the day of wrath..."*
> — Romans 2:5

This is the tragic irony of delay: what you assume is harmless is actually storing up judgment. God's patience is not infinite. It is purposeful.

***

The Days Are Numbered
Scripture does not treat time as limitless.

> *"It is appointed for people to die once—and after this, judgment."*
> — Hebrews 9:27

There is no second life. No reincarnation. No after-death repentance. Once your final breath is taken, your case is sealed.

Jesus told a parable in Luke 12 about a rich man who had everything in life and planned to relax, indulge, and enjoy many more years.

> *"But God said to him, 'You fool! This very night your life is demanded of you.'"*
> — Luke 12:20

That man thought he had time. He didn't.

You may not be promised tomorrow. But you have today. And **today might be your final invitation**.

And that is not a reason to panic—it is a reason to act.

***

Delayed Obedience Is Disobedience

There is a temptation to think that as long as you don't reject God outright, you're in a safe place. But that is not how Scripture speaks.

The same people who heard the truth in Jesus' day and said, "Not yet," were later hardened beyond return.

> *"Today, if you hear His voice, do not harden your hearts."*
> — Hebrews 3:15

That command is not about emotion. It is about responsiveness. If God is speaking—through conviction, Scripture, or circumstance—then the proper response is to yield, immediately.

If you say, "I'll obey when I'm older," you are saying, "I will harden my heart for now and hope it softens later." But the heart does not work that way.

Sin deepens its grip when it is protected. Delay does not preserve opportunity—it erodes it.

***

This Moment Is Mercy

You are not reading this by accident. If you still feel conviction, that is grace. If you still care whether or not you are right with God, that is grace. If you are troubled by the idea of standing before Him in your sin, that is grace.

Conviction is not cruelty. It is evidence that the Spirit of God is still at work in you.

What you do next is not a matter of preference. It is a matter of life and death.

You're still breathing. And that means the door is still open.

But not forever.

Chapter 13

What If I Try and Fail Again?

God knew your weakness before you ever came home.

For many, the barrier to repentance is not disbelief in God's mercy. It's disbelief in their own sincerity.

They've confessed before. They've repented before. They've promised to change—only to fall back into the same sins, the same habits, the same patterns.

And so they ask, honestly: **"What's the point of trying again? What if I fail again?"**

This question doesn't come from defiance. It comes from exhaustion.

They are not mocking grace. They are afraid of abusing it.

And beneath that fear is a quiet despair: **"I don't know how to be faithful."**

That fear is not unfounded. Scripture is honest about human weakness. But it is also clear about divine faithfulness.

Let's address the concern seriously—and biblically.

***

God Knows What You Are
Before God saved you, He already knew your nature.

> *"For he knows how we were formed; He remembers that we are dust.."* — Psalm 103:14

God is not surprised by your struggle. He does not call people to salvation under the illusion that they will then live sinless lives. He calls them knowing exactly what it will take to sanctify them.

The Christian life is not built on the assumption of human strength. It is built on the reality of human weakness and the sufficiency of God's grace.

Paul, who wrote more New Testament letters than anyone, described himself this way:

> *"For I do not do the good that I want to do, but I practice the evil that I do not want to do."*
> — Romans 7:19

This is not an excuse. It is a confession.

Even as a mature believer, Paul acknowledged an ongoing war within himself. He did not present himself as victorious in every moment. He presented himself as **dependent**.

And that is where hope begins.

***

The Christian Life Is a Battle, Not a Showcase

There is a false version of Christianity that promises victory in the form of permanent deliverance from temptation. But

Scripture describes the believer's life in terms of endurance, perseverance, and ongoing struggle.

"Fight the good fight of the faith."
— 1 Timothy 6:12

"Let us run with endurance the race that lies before us." — Hebrews 12:1

"If by the Spirit you put to death the deeds of the body, you will live." — Romans 8:13

None of these commands suggest that failure is impossible. But all of them assume that failure is **not the end**.

Trying and failing is not hypocrisy. **Trying and pretending you don't fail**—that is hypocrisy.

God is not asking you to conquer sin in your own power. He is asking you to walk by the Spirit, to abide in Christ, and to keep coming to Him—not only in strength, but in weakness.

***

Forgiveness Is Not Based on Performance
The question "What if I fail again?" assumes that God's grace is conditional—that it extends only as far as our ability to avoid sin. But that is not how the gospel works.

If your forgiveness depended on your consistency, you would already be lost. But it depends on **Christ's finished work**.

> *"My little children, I am writing you these things*
> *so that you may not sin. But if anyone does sin,*
> *we have an advocate with the Father—Jesus*
> *Christ the righteous one."* — 1 John 2:1

John does not encourage sin. He urges holiness.

But he also knows that believers will fail. And he assures them that Jesus continues to intercede on their behalf.

You may fall again. But you will not fall alone. And you will not fall outside the reach of the One who upholds you.

***

Sanctification Is a Lifelong Process
There is no promise in Scripture that salvation will instantly erase all temptation. There is no guarantee that you will never fall again.

But there is this promise:

> *"He who started a good work in you will carry it*
> *on to completion until the day of Christ Jesus."*
> — Philippians 1:6

God finishes what He starts.

That means your growth in holiness will be slow at times. It will include setbacks. But it will also include progress—real change, real repentance, real spiritual maturity.

And when you fall, He does not cast you away.

"Though a righteous person falls seven times, he will get up." — Proverbs 24:16

The issue is not whether you'll stumble. The issue is whether you'll stay down or rise again in faith.

***

Your Fear Is an Opportunity for Honesty
If you are afraid of repeating your sin, let that fear drive you not into silence, but into clarity.

Ask yourself: Do I hate my sin, or just its consequences? Am I confessing just to feel better, or because I genuinely desire to be made clean?

God is not asking for perfect performance. But He does call for **genuine repentance**.

That means turning from sin—not just in words, but in direction.

And yes, you may still fall. But if you continue to fight—if you continue to seek Him— that fight is itself evidence that the Spirit is working in you.

***

The Gospel Anticipates Your Weakness
Christ did not die for your best moments. He died for your worst.

If you sin again, He will not be surprised. He will not be caught off guard. And He will not revoke what He gave you freely through His blood.

That does not mean you should treat grace lightly. But it means you can treat it **honestly**.

You will fail Him. But He will not fail you.

Even Peter—who cursed and denied Jesus—was met not with wrath, but breakfast and restoration on the shore (John 21). Jesus didn't just forgive him. He recommissioned him.

> *"The one who comes to Me I will never cast out."*
> — John 6:37

If you come again—honestly, humbly, truly— He will receive you again.

Chapter 14
You Can Come Home Today
No more waiting. No more excuses. The door is still open.

There's a moment in every story when the door is still open. Before the sun sets. Before the judgment falls. Before the sentence is carried out. A window remains. You're in that moment now. Not by chance. Not by your own design. But by the mercy of a God who is slow to anger and full of compassion.

You don't have to die and go to hell. Not because hell isn't real. Not because sin isn't serious. But because God has made a way—and that way is still open to you.

***

The Father Is Not Finished
Jesus once told a story about a young man who left home, wasted everything, and hit rock bottom. In shame and hunger, he finally decided to go home—not to ask for restoration, but to beg for mercy. He had no illusions of earning anything.

But while he was still far off, the father saw him. And the father ran. He didn't wait for groveling. He didn't demand explanations. He embraced the son. He called for a robe and a ring. He celebrated—not because the boy got everything right, but because he came home.

> *"For this son of mine was dead and is alive again; he was lost and is found!"* —Luke 15:24

That is not just a parable. It is the heart of God toward you. You may have wandered far. You may have wasted years. But the Father is watching. And He still wants you.

***

You Don't Have to Stay Where You Are
No matter how deep the pit, God's arm is not too short to save.

> *"Come, let us settle this," says the LORD. "Though your sins are scarlet, they will be as white as snow."* —Isaiah 1:18

That promise is not reserved for the clean or the religious or the successful. It is for sinners. Stubborn sinners. Dirty sinners. People who know they've blown it more than once.

There is no halfway gospel. There is no partial pardon. Christ didn't shed His blood to make you almost forgiven. He came to remove the entire record of sin and give you His righteousness.

You don't have to stay in shame. You don't have to pretend. You don't have to delay. You can come home.

***

But You Must Decide
Joshua once stood before the people and said:

> *"Choose for yourselves today: Who will you serve?"* —Joshua 24:15

The same choice stands before you now. Not because this book says so, but because God Himself has laid the path of life before you.

You cannot walk both roads. You cannot cling to sin and claim the Savior. You cannot serve two masters. But you can choose. You can choose the One who already chose to love you. You can choose to serve the Lord.

***

The Response God Calls For

There are really two kinds of people reading this right now.

Some of you have already been baptized into Christ. You believed the gospel. You obeyed His call. You were buried with Him and raised to walk in new life. But somewhere along the way, you wandered.

This moment isn't about getting baptized again. It's about coming back to the One who baptized you with His Spirit and sealed you as His own.

If that's you—what God calls for now is repentance. A turning. A coming home.

> *"If we confess our sins, He is faithful and just to forgive us our sins and to cleanse us from all unrighteousness."* —1 John 1:9

> *"Return to Me," declares the LORD, "and I will return to you."* —Malachi 3:7

Others of you have never truly responded to the gospel.
You may believe in God. You may have prayed before. But
you've never turned from sin. You've never been immersed
into Christ. You've never had your sins washed away.

The Bible is clear about what God expects:

> *"Repent and be baptized, each of you, in the
> name of Jesus Christ for the forgiveness of your
> sins..."* —Acts 2:38

> *"And now, why are you delaying? Get up and be
> baptized, and wash away your sins, calling on
> His name."* —Acts 22:16

This is not about checking a box. It's about surrender. Faith
that hears and obeys. Repentance that turns from sin. Baptism
that unites you with Christ and clothes you in His name.

If you've never done that—don't wait. You don't have to
clean yourself up first. You just need to come.

Your window is open now. Walk through it while there's still
time.

***

You've Heard the Truth
You've seen what Scripture says. You've faced the weight of
judgment. You've heard the offer of grace. You've read about
the cross, the resurrection, the mercy of God, and the way
home.

Now it's your move—because this isn't just about this moment. It's about eternity. Don't look to your feelings. Don't wait for a sign. Don't assume there will be another chance. If you hear His voice today, don't harden your heart.

You can talk to Him right now. Not with perfect words. Just with a real heart.

If you are a prodigal—come home with repentance.

You can pray as David did—broken, honest, and ready to come home:

> *"God, I have sinned against You. I don't make excuses. I don't hide. I know my guilt. I feel the weight of it.*
>
> *But I believe You are full of mercy. Wash me. Cleanse me. Make me new.*
>
> *Create in me a clean heart, O God. Renew a steadfast spirit within me.*
>
> *Don't cast me away. Don't give up on me. Restore to me the joy of Your salvation.*
>
> *I want to follow You. I want to be Yours. And if You heal me—I'll help others come home too."*

It's not the words that save. It's the Christ you run to. But when you come to Him like David did—broken, honest, and humbled—God listens. He's not looking for perfect phrases. He wants your heart poured out like water, your soul laid bare.

A broken and contrite heart, He will not despise. And when you truly run to Him—He will not turn you away.

You don't have to die and go to hell. You don't have to be defined by failure. You don't have to guess where you stand with God. You don't have to hide, pretend, or clean yourself up first. You can come home today.

And when you do, you'll find the Father already running toward you.

Chapter 15

Choose Life

"I call heaven and earth as witnesses against you today: that I have set before you life and death, blessing and curse. So choose life, so that you and your children may live." — Deuteronomy 30:19

This was Moses' final message to a people who had wandered for forty years. They had seen miracles. They had heard God's voice. They had failed more than once. And yet—God was still offering them life.

That same offer still stands. Not because you've earned it. Not because you deserve it. But because God still desires to show mercy.

***

You Know the Truth Now

No one who finishes this book can say, "I didn't know." You've seen the warnings. You've heard the gospel. You've walked through sin, judgment, mercy, the cross, the empty tomb, and the open invitation.

Now you know what's at stake. And now it's your move.

Life or death. Blessing or curse. Obedience or rebellion. Christ or yourself. Heaven or hell.

You can't hold both. You must choose.

And make no mistake: **Not choosing is a choice.**

***

Your Life Will Shape Others

Moses didn't just say, "Choose life for yourself." He said, *"so that you and your children may live."*

Your choice will ripple outward. You don't live in isolation.

What you believe will shape your family. What you value will lead your friends. What you chase will teach your children what matters. How you walk will either shine light—or add to the darkness.

You don't get to decide who sees your life. But you do get to decide what they see when they look at you.

And someday, your children—or your neighbors, or your spouse, or someone you never realized was watching—may stand at their own crossroads and ask,

> *"Was life really an option?"*

Let them know by your example that it was.

***

The Door Is Still Open—But It Won't Stay That Way Forever

Moses gave that final plea on the edge of the Promised Land. He would die soon after. And many of the people would turn back to idols.

They had been warned. They had been offered life. But many still chose death.

God won't force you to love Him. He won't drag you into heaven. He won't override your will.

He will stand in front of you, arms open, and say:

"Choose life."

And if you do—you'll find that He's already gone ahead of you to prepare the way.

***

One Final Word

If you're holding this book, and you still haven't decided—Let this be your moment.

Don't wait until it's comfortable. Don't wait until you understand everything. Don't wait until you "feel ready."

That day may never come. But this day is here.

And the Lord of heaven and earth, who formed you, saw you, and died for you, is still saying:

Choose life.

Not tomorrow. Not someday. **Today.**

Because you don't have to die and go to hell. But you **do** have to decide.

Addendum
What Must I Do to Be Saved?

You may be asking:

"Am I really saved? What do I need to do?"

That is not just an important question—it is the most important question a person can ask.

It was asked in Scripture more than once.

In Acts 2, when Peter preached that the crowd had crucified the Son of God, the people were "cut to the heart" and cried out,

> *"Brothers, what shall we do?"* — Acts 2:37

In Acts 16, a Philippian jailer fell trembling before Paul and Silas after an earthquake shook the prison open. He asked:

> *"What must I do to be saved?"* — Acts 16:30

God has answered that question — clearly, consistently, and repeatedly — in His Word. And the answer hasn't changed.

Born Innocent — Separated by Sin
Every child is born pure and good, made in the image of God. Jesus Himself said, "Unless you become like little children, you will never enter the kingdom of heaven" (Matthew 18:3). We are not born guilty — but we do eventually choose sin. Like Adam and Eve, we reach a point when we know what is right and we go our own way.

The Bible says,

> *"All have sinned and fall short of the glory of God."*
> — Romans 3:23

And again,

> *"Your iniquities have separated you from your God."*
> — Isaiah 59:2

Sin is not just a mistake. It is rebellion. It severs our relationship with a holy God—and we cannot fix that on our own. That's why Jesus came.

Jesus Died to Save You

"While we were still sinners, Christ died for us." (Romans 5:8) God's grace is not earned. It is not deserved. It is offered freely because of what Jesus did on the cross. He took our place. He bore our guilt. He made a way home.

But even though Jesus died for everyone, not everyone is saved. His blood must be received—not by ritual, not by good works, but by obedient faith. And Scripture shows us exactly how.

The Response God Calls For

Every conversion in the book of Acts follows the same pattern: people heard the gospel, and they responded with belief, repentance, confession, and baptism.

1. Believe in Jesus Christ

Faith is the foundation. We must believe that Jesus is the Son of God—that He lived, died, and rose again. Without that trust, there can be no salvation.

> *"Without faith it is impossible to please God."*
> —Hebrews 11:6

> *"Whoever believes and is baptized will be saved."*
> —Mark 16:16

But belief alone isn't enough. Even the demons believe—and tremble (James 2:19). True biblical faith always leads to action.

2. Repent of Your Sins

To repent means to turn. It's not just feeling sorry—it's a change of heart that leads to a change of direction. You stop running your own way and start following Jesus.

> *"Repent and be baptized... for the forgiveness of your sins."* — Acts 2:38

Some people want salvation without surrender. But Jesus said,

> *"If anyone would come after Me, he must deny himself, take up his cross, and follow Me."*
> —Luke 9:23

3. Confess Jesus as Lord

Saving faith is never silent. When you believe in Jesus, you speak it. You declare Him as Lord of your life.

"If you confess with your mouth, 'Jesus is Lord,' and believe in your heart that God raised Him from the dead, you will be saved." — Romans 10:9

In Acts 8, the Ethiopian man said,

> *"I believe that Jesus Christ is the Son of God."*
> — Acts 8:37

This is not a one-time statement, but the beginning of a life lived in allegiance to Jesus.

4. Be Baptized Into Christ

This is the step where many modern teachings fall short. But the New Testament leaves no doubt: baptism is the moment when saving faith becomes complete.

It is not a symbol of something that has already happened—it is the moment it happens.

In Acts 2:38, Peter said,

> *"Repent and be baptized, every one of you, in the name of Jesus Christ for the forgiveness of your sins, and you will receive the gift of the Holy Spirit."*

In Romans 6, Paul describes baptism as a burial:

> *"We were buried with Him through baptism into death, so that just as Christ was raised from the dead, we too may live a new life."* — Romans 6:4

When we are immersed in water, we are united with Christ's death. Our old life is crucified. We are raised with Him to walk in newness of life.

Colossians 2:12–13 says we are *"buried with Him in baptism"* and that it is in that moment God *"made [us] alive with Christ"* and *"forgave us all our sins."*

In Galatians 3:27, Paul writes,

> *"For all of you who were baptized into Christ have clothed yourselves with Christ."*

We are not clothed with Christ simply by believing in Him. Baptism is how we are united with Him, clothed in His righteousness, and added to His family.

Peter makes it even clearer:

> *"Baptism now saves you — not the removal of dirt from the body but the pledge of a clear conscience toward God."* — 1 Peter 3:21

And when Saul of Tarsus (later known as Paul) was convicted of his sin, Ananias told him plainly:

> *"And now, what are you waiting for? Get up, be baptized and wash your sins away, calling on His name."* — Acts 22:16

There is no confusion here. Baptism is the moment of salvation—the place where grace is received, sins are washed away, and the Holy Spirit is given.

After Baptism — Keep Walking in the Light

You won't be perfect after baptism. None of us are. But the Bible says:

> *"But if we walk in the light, as he is in the light, we have fellowship with one another, and the blood of Jesus his Son cleanses us from all sin."* — 1 John 1:7

The verb "cleanses" is present tense—He keeps washing you as you stay in the light. You don't get re-baptized every time you stumble. You confess, repent, and keep walking. He is faithful.

God's Plan—Simple and Beautiful

What must I do to be saved?

The Bible's answer is not complicated. It's not buried in church tradition or opinion. It's right there on the pages of Scripture:

Hear the gospel (Romans 10:17)
Believe in Jesus Christ (John 8:24)
Repent of your sins (Acts 17:30)
Confess Jesus as Lord (Romans 10:9–10)
Be baptized for the forgiveness of sins (Acts 2:38; Romans 6:3–4)
Live faithfully in the light of His grace (Revelation 2:10)

Not to earn salvation—but to receive it on God's terms, not ours.

So What Are You Waiting For?

If you've never obeyed the gospel...

If you've believed in Jesus but never been baptized for the forgiveness of sins...

If you've been told baptism is "just a symbol"...

Search the Scriptures.

Let God speak.

Obey the gospel.

> *"And now, what are you waiting for? Get up, be baptized and wash your sins away, calling on His name."* — Acts 22:16

He's ready.

The water is ready.

And your new life can begin.

Discussion Questions

For Personal Reflection or Group Study

Whether you're reading this alone or with others, take time to slow down and reflect. Let these questions guide you into prayer, journaling, and honest conversation with God.

If you're working through this as a group or class, use each question as a way to teach, encourage, and grow together.

Be open. Be real. Let this be more than a study—let it be a space where Jesus meets you to heal, restore, and renew.

When Jesus stood in the synagogue in Luke 4, He read from the scroll of Isaiah and declared, "Today this Scripture is fulfilled in your hearing." What He read was this:

"The Spirit of the Lord GOD is upon me,
because the LORD has anointed me
to bring good news to the poor;
he has sent me to bind up the brokenhearted,
to proclaim liberty to the captives,
and the opening of the prison to those who are bound;
to proclaim the year of the LORD's favor...
to comfort all who mourn...
to give them a beautiful headdress instead of ashes,
the oil of gladness instead of mourning,
the garment of praise instead of a faint spirit."
— Isaiah 61:1–3

That's the heart behind these questions. Let them lead you into the presence of the One who came not just to teach, but to transform.

Chapter 1 – Hell Wasn't Meant for You

- What have you heard about hell before? Where did those ideas come from—Scripture, culture, tradition, or fear?

  _____

  _____

  _____

  _____

- Why is it significant to realize that hell was not created for people?

  _____

  _____

  _____

  _____

- _Read Matthew 25:41._ Who was hell originally prepared for, and why does that matter?

  _____

  _____

  _____

  _____

- How does knowing God didn't design hell for you affect how you see His justice?

_____

_____

_____

_____

Chapter 2 – I'm Too Far Gone

- Have you ever felt like you crossed a line God couldn't forgive?

  _____

  _____

  _____

  _____

- What does your reaction to your own failure say about what you believe about grace?

  _____

  _____

  _____

  _____

- _Read Luke 15:11–24._ How does the father respond before the son finishes his apology?

  _____

  _____

  _____

  _____

- What parts of the parable challenge your assumptions about God's mercy?

  _____

  _____

  _____

  _____

Chapter 3 – I Was Baptized...Then Blew It

- Why is it so easy to believe that failure after baptism cancels your salvation?

  _____

  _____

  _____

  _____

- _Read Romans 8:1._ What does this say about condemnation for those in Christ?

  _____

  _____

  _____

  _____

- How should we understand baptism, restoration, and continued repentance?

  _____

  _____

  _____

  _____

- Have you ever let shame keep you from returning to God? Why?

_____

_____

_____

_____

Chapter 4 – I Don't Feel Forgiven

- What do you usually rely on more—God's Word or your emotions?

  _____

  _____

  _____

  _____

- *Read 1 John 1:9.* What does it say God will do if we confess?

  _____

  _____

  _____

  _____

- Why is it dangerous to let feelings define whether you believe you're forgiven?

  _____

  _____

  _____

  _____

- How can you tell the difference between godly conviction and toxic shame?

  _____

  _____

  _____

  _____

- What helps you preach truth to yourself when shame lingers?

  _____

  _____

  _____

  _____

Chapter 5 – I Think I Missed My Chance

- Have you ever felt like God gave you an opportunity—and you blew it?

  _____

  _____

  _____

  _____

- _Read 2 Peter 3:9._ What does this verse teach about God's patience?

  _____

  _____

  _____

  _____

- What does the thief on the cross show us about how late grace can still reach?

  _____

  _____

  _____

  _____

- If you feel regret, does that mean God is finished with you—or still calling?

  _____

  _____

  _____

  _____

Chapter 6 – Success Isn't Salvation

- What are some things people chase that can distract them from pursuing God?

  _____

  _____

  _____

  _____

- *Read Mark 8:36–37.* What does Jesus say about gaining the world but losing your soul?

  _____

  _____

  _____

  _____

- Why is it dangerous to let success or recognition become the focus of your life?

  _____

  _____

  _____

  _____

- How can unresolved pain, anger, or bitterness also pull your heart away from God?

  _____

  _____

  _____

  _____

- *Read Matthew 6:21.* What does this verse reveal about how your priorities reveal your heart?

  _____

  _____

  _____

  _____

- What does it look like to lay down your "treasures" and return your heart to God?

  _____

  _____

  _____

  _____

Chapter 7 – Jesus Took Your Place

- What does it mean that Jesus died as your substitute—not just an example?

  _____

  _____

  _____

  _____

- _Read Isaiah 53:5–6._ What specific things did Jesus carry in our place?

  _____

  _____

  _____

  _____

- Why was it necessary for judgment to fall on someone—and why was it Him?

  _____

  _____

  _____

  _____

- How does the truth of substitution change the way you respond to sin?

  _____

  _____

  _____

  _____

Chapter 8 – God Wants You

- Why is it hard to believe that God actually wants you—not just forgives you?

  _____

  _____

  _____

  _____

- *Read Romans 5:8.* What does this say about the timing and depth of God's love?

  _____

  _____

  _____

  _____

- What does it mean that salvation is not reluctant mercy, but deliberate love?

  _____

  _____

  _____

  _____

- How can your view of God's desire for you reshape your identity?

_____

_____

_____

_____

Chapter 9 – The Gift You Must Choose

- What does it mean that salvation is a gift, not a transaction?

  _____

  _____

  _____

  _____

- *Read John 1:12.* What's the condition for becoming God's child?

  _____

  _____

  _____

  _____

- Why is refusal to respond not neutral—but a rejection of grace?

  _____

  _____

  _____

  _____

- What's stopping you—or someone you know—from receiving that gift?

  _____

  _____

  _____

  _____

- What are the dangers of waiting too long to respond to the gospel?

  _____

  _____

  _____

  _____

Chapter 10 – What Does God Want From Me Now?

- After being saved, what does God actually expect from your daily life?

  _____

  _____

  _____

  _____

- *Read Romans 12:1–2.* What does it mean to offer your body as a living sacrifice?

  _____

  _____

  _____

  _____

- How can obedience be an act of worship rather than duty?

  _____

  _____

  _____

  _____

- Why is the local church essential for your growth—
  not optional?

  _____

  _____

  _____

  _____

Chapter 11 – Forgiven, But Not Untouched

- What's a consequence from your past that still lingers today?

  _____

  _____

  _____

  _____

- Why do you think we often expect forgiveness to undo all the damage of sin?

  _____

  _____

  _____

  _____

- _Read 2 Samuel 12:13–14._ How do we see both God's mercy and justice in His response to David?

  _____

  _____

  _____

  _____

- What does it look like to live free from guilt, but still honest about the scars?

  _____

  _____

  _____

  _____

- *Read Psalm 51:3 and Proverbs 6:32–33.* What truths do these verses reveal about memory, regret, and redemption?

  _____

  _____

  _____

  _____

Chapter 12 – Why You're Still Breathing

- What does each day of life say about God's patience with you?

  _____

  _____

  _____

  _____

- *Read Romans 2:4.* How is kindness meant to lead us to repentance?

  _____

  _____

  _____

  _____

- Why is delay dangerous when it comes to responding to God?

  _____

  _____

  _____

  _____

- How has God preserved your life to give you space to come home?

  _____

  _____

  _____

  _____

- How has your personal story intersected with God's mercy?

  _____

  _____

  _____

  _____

Chapter 13 – What If I Try and Fail Again?

- What fears make you hesitate to fully surrender to God?

  _____

  _____

  _____

  _____

- *Read 1 John 2:1–2.* What role does Jesus play after we sin again?

  _____

  _____

  _____

  _____

- How does grace differ from permission?

  _____

  _____

  _____

  _____

- Why is trying and failing different from refusing to fight at all?

  _____

  _____

  _____

  _____

- What evidence in your life shows the Spirit is still working in you—even when you fall?

  _____

  _____

  _____

  _____

Chapter 14 – You Can Come Home Today

- What's stopping you from coming home to God today?

  _____

  _____

  _____

  _____

- _Read Deuteronomy 30:19._ What does it mean to "choose life"?

  _____

  _____

  _____

  _____

- How do you know the invitation is still open?

  _____

  _____

  _____

  _____

- If you believe you've waited too long, what evidence does the gospel give that you haven't?

_____

_____

_____

_____

Chapter 15 – Choose Life

- What stood out to you most in Moses' call to "choose life" in *Deuteronomy 30:19*?

  _____

  _____

  _____

  _____

- What's the difference between knowing about the truth and choosing it?

  _____

  _____

  _____

  _____

- How does your choice today shape the lives of others around you?

  _____

  _____

  _____

  _____

- What does procrastination look like in your faith? What's one way to act now?

  _____

  _____

  _____

  _____

- How can you help others make this choice—and keep walking in it daily?

  _____

  _____

  _____

  _____

When You Feel Unforgivable
Scriptures to Read

If you've ever felt too far gone—too guilty, too stained, too broken—these verses are for you. They aren't church talk or motivational quotes. They are God's own words, speaking straight into your shame and calling you back to grace. Let them wash over you. Let them hold you. Let them prove that forgiveness is still on the table.

***

Return to me, and I will return to you. *Malachi 3:7*

I, yes I, am the one who wipes out your transgressions for my own sake, and I will not remember your sins. *Isaiah 43:25*

Come now, let's settle this, says the LORD. Though your sins are like scarlet, they will be as white as snow. *Isaiah 1:18*

As far as the east is from the west, so far has he removed our transgressions from us. *Psalm 103:12*

A broken and contrite heart, O God, you will not despise. *Psalm 51:17*

Though I fall, I will rise; though I sit in darkness, the LORD will be my light. *Micah 7:8*

You threw all my sins behind your back. *Isaiah 38:17*

He will again have compassion on us; he will vanquish our iniquities. You will cast all our sins into the depths of the sea. *Micah 7:19*

The LORD is close to the brokenhearted and saves those who are crushed in spirit. *Psalm 34:18*

If we confess our sins, he is faithful and righteous to forgive us our sins and to cleanse us from all unrighteousness. *1 John 1:9*

There is now no condemnation for those who are in Christ Jesus. *Romans 8:1*

While we were still sinners, Christ died for us. *Romans 5:8*

Everyone the Father gives me will come to me, and the one who comes to me I will never cast out. *John 6:37*

Even if our hearts condemn us, God is greater than our hearts. *1 John 3:20*

About the author

Dennis Wilson grew up in a Deaf household—the son of parents who came to Christ later in life and never looked back. That foundation—a faith shaped through trial and sustained by grace—has shaped his life and message ever since.

A preacher, missionary, and Bible instructor, Dennis has spent decades helping people meet Jesus—not through hype or performance, but through truth that confronts, heals, and restores. He has preached in English, Spanish, and American Sign Language. He's been a houseparent to the fatherless, a teacher to the hungry, and a steady voice to the wandering.

From mission work in Russia and Mexico to quiet conversations in American living rooms, Dennis has walked with people through sin, sorrow, and salvation—always pointing them home to the Father.

He currently serves as an instructor for the Deaf at Sunset International Bible Institute, where he trains others to share the gospel clearly and faithfully.

Dennis believes everyone should have access to the truth—whether they've never heard it before or have walked away and wondered if they can come back. **This book is for them.**

If you have questions or need someone to talk to, Dennis would love to hear from you:

dennis@straighttruthpress.com

For Personal Notes

"Come to Me, all of you who are weary and burdened, and I will give you rest. Take my yoke upon you and learn from me, because I am gentle and humble in heart, and you will find rest for your souls. For my yoke is easy and my burden is light."

— Matthew 11:28–30
Yoked Translation